I0421224

The Philosophy of Despair

by David Starr Jordan

Copyright © 8/14/2015
Jefferson Publication

ISBN-13: 978-1516907410

Printed in the United States of America

The Bubbles of Sáki.

From Fitzgerald's exquisite version of the Rubáiyát of
Omar Khayyám, I take the following quatrains which
may serve as a text for what I have to say:

So when the angel of the darker Drink
At last shall find you by the river-brink,
And offering you his cup, invite your Soul
Forth to your lips to quaff, you shall not shrink.

Why, if the soul can fling the Dust aside,
And naked on the air of Heaven ride,
Wert not a shame—wert not a shame for him
In this clay carcase crippled to abide?

'Tis but a tent where takes his one-day's rest
A Sultan to the realm of Death addrest;
The Sultan rises, and the dark Ferrásh
Strikes, and prepares it for another guest.

And fear not lest Existence, closing your
Account, and mine, shall know the like no more;
The Eternal Sáki from that bowl hath pour'd
Millions of bubbles like us, and will pour.

When you and I behind the veil are past,
Oh, but the long, long while the world shall last,
Which of our coming and departure heeds
As the Sev'n Seas shall heed a pebble-cast.

A moment's halt—a momentary taste
Of Being from the Well amid the waste,
And lo!—the phantom caravan has reach'd
The Nothing it set out from—O, make haste!

* * *

There was the door to which I found no key;
There was the veil through which I could not see:
Some little talk awhile of Me and Thee
There was—and then no more of Thee and Me.

* * *

Why, all the Saints and Sages who discuss'd
Of the two worlds so learnedly are thrust
Like foolish prophets forth; their words to scorn
Are scatter'd and their mouths are stopt with dust.

With them the seed of wisdom did I sow,
And with my own hand wrought to make it grow
And this was all the harvest that I reap'd—
"I come like water, and like wind I go."

* * *

Ah Love, could thou and I with Him conspire
To grasp this sorry scheme of Things entire,
Would we not shatter it to bits—and then
Re-mould it nearer to the heart's desire!

Yon rising Moon that looks for us again—
How oft hereafter will she wax and wane;

How oft hereafter rising look for us
Through this same garden—and for one in vain!

And when like her, O Sáki, you shall pass
Among the guests, star-scattered on the grass,
And in your blissful errand reach the spot
Where I made one—turn down an empty glass!

* * *

And, again, in another poem from Carmen Silva's
Roumanian folk-songs:

Hopeless.

Into the mist I gazed, and fear came on me,
Then said the mist: "I weep for the lost sun."

We sat beneath our tent;
Then he that hath no hope drew near us there,
And sat him down by us.
We asked him: "Hast thou seen the plains, the
mountains?"
And he made answer: "I have seen them all."
And then his cloak he showed us, and his shirt,
Torn was the shirt, there, close above the heart,
Pierced was the breast, there, close above the heart—
The heart was gone.
And yet he trembled not, the while we looked,
And sought the heart, the heart that was not there.
He let us look. And he that had no hope
Smiled, that we grew so pale, and sang us songs.
Then we did envy him, that he could sing
Without a heart to suffer what he sang.

And when he went, he cast his cloak about him,
And those that met him, they could never guess
How that his shirt was torn about the heart,
And that his breast was pierced above the heart,
And that the heart was gone.

I gazed into the mist, and fear came on me,
Then said the mist: "I weep for the lost sun."

This poem of Omar and of Fitzgerald is perhaps our best expression of the sadness and the grandeur of insoluble problems. It is the sweetness of philosophical sorrow which has no kinship with misery or distress. In the strains of the saddest music the soul finds the keenest delight. The same sweet, sorrowful pleasure is felt in the play of the mind about the riddles which it cannot solve.

In the presence of the infinite problem of life, the voice of Science is dumb, for Science is the coördinate and corrected expression of human experience, and human experience must stop with the limitations of human life. Man was not present "When the foundations of the Earth were laid," and beyond the certainty that they were laid in wisdom and power, man can say little about them. Man finds in the economy of nature "no trace of a beginning; no prospect of an end!" He may feel sure, with Hutton, that "time is as long as space is wide." But he cannot conceive of space as actually without limit, nor can he imagine any limiting conditions. He cannot think of a period before time began, nor of a state in which time shall be no more. The mind fails before the idea of time's eternal continuity. So time becomes to man merely the sequence of the earthly events in which he and his ancestors have taken part. Even thus limited it is sadly immortal, while man's stay on the earth is but of "few days and full of trouble." "Oh, but the long, long while this world shall last!" or as the grim humorist puts it, "we shall be a long time dead."

Though the meaning of time, space, existence lies beyond our reach, yet some sort of solution of the infinite problem the human heart demands. We find in life a power for action, limited though this power may be. Life is action, and action is impossible if devoid of motive or hope.

It is my purpose here to indicate some part of the answer of Science to the Philosophy of Despair. Direct reply Science has none. We cannot argue against a singer or a poet. The poet sings of what he feels, but Science speaks only of what we know. We feel infinity, but we cannot know it, for to the highest human wisdom the ultimate truths of the universe are no nearer than to the child. Science knows no ultimate truths. These are beyond the reach of man, and all that man knows must be stated in terms of his experience. But as to human experience and conduct, Science has a word to say.

Therefore Science can speak of the causes and results of Pessimism. It can touch the practical side of the riddle of life by asking certain questions, the answers to which lie within the province of human experience. Among these are the following:

Why is there a "Philosophy of Despair?"

Can Despair be wrought into healthful life?

In what part of the Universe are you and what are you doing?

Personal despair or discouragement may rise from failure of strength or failure of plans. This is a matter of every-day occurrence. The "best laid schemes o' mice and men" generally go wrong, no doubt, but this fact has little to do with the Philosophy of Pessimism. It is natural for mice and men to try again and to gain wisdom from failures. "By the embers of loss we count our gains."

The Pessimism of Youth we may first consider: In the transition from childhood to manhood great changes take place in the nervous system. There is for a time a period of confusion, in which the nerve cells are acquiring new powers and new relations. This is followed by a time of joy and exuberance, a sense of a new life in a new world, a feeling of new power and adequacy, the thought that life is richer and better worth living than the child could have supposed.

To this in turn comes a feeling of reaction. The joys of life have been a thousand times felt before they come to us. We are but following part of a cut-and-dried program, "performing actions and reciting speeches made up for us centuries before we were born." The new power of manhood and womanhood which seemed so wonderful find their close limitations. As our own part in the Universe seems to shrink as we take our place in it, so does the Universe itself seem to grow small, hard and unsympathetic. Very few young men or young women of strength and feeling fail to pass through a period of Pessimism. With some it is merely an affectation caught from the cheap literature of decadence. It then may find expression in imitation, as a few years ago the sad-hearted youth turned down his collar in sympathy with the "conspicuous loneliness" that took the starch out of the collar of Byron. "The youth," says Zangwill, "says bitter things about Life which Life would have winced to hear had it been alive." With others Pessimism has deeper roots and finds its expression in the poetry or philosophy of real despair.

This adolescent Pessimism cannot be wrought into action. The mood disappears when real action is demanded. The Pessimism of youth vanishes with the coming of life. Through the rush of the new century, the fad of the drooping spirit has already given way to the fad of the strenuous life. Equally unreasoning it may be, but far more wholesome.

But if action is impossible, the mood remains. And here arises the despair of the highly educated. The purpose of knowledge is action. But to refuse action is to secure time for the acquisition of more knowledge. It is written in the very structure of the brain that each impression of the senses must bring with it the impulse to act. To resist this impulse is in turn to destroy it and to substitute a dull soul-ache in its place. "Much study is a weariness of the flesh, and the experience of all the ages brings only despair if it cannot be wrought into life. This lack of balance between knowledge and achievement is the main element in a form of ineffectiveness which with various others has been uncritically called Degeneration. As the common pleasures which arise from active life become impossible or distasteful, the desire for more intense and novel joys comes in, and with the goading of the thirst for these comes ever deeper discouragement.

At the best, the tendency of large knowledge, not vitalized by practical experience, is to spend itself in cynical criticism, in futile efforts to tear down without feeling the higher obligation to build up. For it is the essence of this form of Pessimism to feel that there is nothing on earth worth the trouble of building. The real is only a "sneering comment" on the ideal, and man's life is too short to make any action worth while.

"With her the seed of Wisdom did I sow,
And with mine own hands wrought to make it grow;
And this is all the harvest that I reap'd,
'I come like water, and like wind I go.'"

One of the few things that we may know in life is this, that it is impossible for man to know anything absolutely. The power of reasoning is a mere "by-product in the process of Evolution." It is but an instrument to help out the confusion of the senses, and it is conditioned by the accuracy of the sense-perceptions with which it deals. There is no appeal from experience to reason, for reason is powerless to act save on the facts of human experience. Speculative philosophy can teach us nothing. The senses and the reason are intensely practical and all, our faculties are primarily adapted to immediate purposes. Instruments such as these cannot serve to probe the nature of the infinite. But no other instruments lie within reach of man. If we cannot "reach the heart of reality" by reason, what indeed can we reach? What right have we to know or to believe? And if we can know or believe nothing, what should we try to do? And how indeed can we do anything? Every man's fate is determined by his heredity and his environment. In the Arab proverb he is born with his fate bound to his neck. In the course of life we must do that which has been already cut out for us. Our parts were laid for us long before we appeared to take them. He is indeed a strong man who can vary the cast or give a different cue to those who follow. Nature is no respecter of persons, and to suppose that any man is in any degree "the arbiter of his own destiny" is pure illusion. We are thrust forth into life, against our will. Against our will we are forced to leave it. We find ourselves, as has been said, "on a steep incline, where we can veer but little to the left or right"; whichever way we move we fall finally to the very bottom. The fires we kindle die away in coals; castles we build vanish before our eyes. The river sinks in the sands of the desert. The character we form by our efforts disintegrates in spite of our effort. If life be spared we find ourselves once again helpless children. Whichever way we turn we may describe the course of life in metaphors of discouragement.

To the pessimistic philosopher the progress of the race is also mere illusion. There is no progress, only adaptation. Every creature must fit itself to its environment or pass away. The beast fits the forest for the same reason that the river fits its bed. Life is only possible under the rare conditions in which life is not destroyed.

In such fashion we may ring the changes of the despair of philosophy. If we are to take up the threads of life by the farther end only, we shall never begin to live, for only those which lie next us can ever be in our hand. To grasp at ultimate truth is to be forever empty-handed. To reach for the ultimate end of action is never to begin to act.

Deeper and more worthy of respect is the sadness of science. The effort "to see things as they really are," to get out of all make-believe and to secure that "absolute veracity of thought" without which sound action is impossible does not always lead to hopefulness.

There is much to discourage in human history,—in the facts of human life. The common man, after all the ages, is still very common. He is ignorant, reckless, unjust, selfish, easily misled. All public affairs bear the stamp of his weakness. Especially is this shown in the prevalence of destructive strife. The boasted progress of civilization is dissolved in the barbarism of war. Whether glory or conquest or commercial greed be war's purpose, the ultimate result of war is death. Its essential feature is the slaughter of the young, the brave, the ambitious, the hopeful, leaving the weak, the sickly, the discouraged to perpetuate the race. Thus all militant, nations become decadent ones. Thus the glory of Rome, her conquests and her splendor of achievement, left the Romans at home a nation of cowards, and such they are to this day. For those who survive are not the sons of the Romans, but of the slaves, scullions, the idlers and camp-followers whom the years of Roman glory could not use and did not destroy. War blasts and withers all that is worthy in the works of man.

That there seems no way out of this is the cause of the sullen despair of so many scholars of Continental Europe.

The millennium is not in sight. It is farther away than fifty years ago. The future is narrowing down and men do not care to forecast it. It is enough to grasp what we may of the present. We hear "the ring of the hammer on the scaffold." "Let us eat and drink, for tomorrow we die." "The sad kings," in Watson's phrase, can only pile up fuel for their own destruction, and the failure of force will release the unholy brood which force has caused to develop. The winds of freedom are tainted by sulphurous exhalations. In all our merry-making we find with Ibsen that "there is a corpse on board." The mask is falling only to show the Death's head there concealed. Aristocracy, Democracy, Anarchy, Empire, the history of politics, is the eternal round of the Dance of Death.

When we look at human nature in detail we find more of animal than of angel, and the "veracity of thought and action," which is the choicest gift of Science, is lost in the happy-go-lucky movement of the human mob. "To see things as they really are" is the purpose of the philosophy of Pessimism in the hands of its worthiest exponents. But we know what is, and that alone, even were such knowledge possible, is not to know the truth. The higher wisdom seeks to find the forces at work to produce that which now is. The present time is the meeting time of forces; the present fact their temporary product. To the philosophy of Evolution, "every meanest day is the conflux of two eternities." Each meanest fact is the product of the world forces that lie behind it; each meanest man the resultant of the vast powers, alive in human nature, struggling since life began. And these forces, omnipotent and eternal, will never cease their work.

To the philosophy of Pessimism, the child is a mere human larva, weak, perverse, disagreeable, the heir of mortality, with all manner of "defects of doubt and taints of blood," gathered in the long experience of its wretched parentage.

In the more hopeful view of Evolution the child exists for its possibilities. The huge forces within have thrown it to the surface of time. They will push it onward to development, which may not be much in the individual case, but beyond it all lie the possibilities of its race. Inherent in it is the power to rise, to form its own environment, to stand at last superior to the blind forces by which the human will was made. With this thought is sure to come, in some degree, the certainty that the heart of the Universe is sound, that though there be so many of us in the world, each must have his place, and each at last "be somehow needful to infinity." We can see that each least creature has its need for being. The present justifies the past. It is the transcendent future which renders the commonplace present possible.

The "dragons of the prime,
That tore each other in the slime,"

lived and fought that we their descendants may realize ourselves in "lives made beautiful and sweet," through all unlikeness to dragons. It was necessary that every foot of soil in Europe should be crimsoned by blood, wantonly shed, to bring the relative peace and tolerance of the civilization of Europe today. It always "needs that offense must come" to bring about the better condition in which each particular offense shall be done away. For the evolution of life is not in straight lines from lower to higher things, but runs rather in wavering spirals. It is the resultant of stress and storm. The evil and failure which darken the present are necessary to the illumination of the future. Time is long. "God tosses back to man his failures" one by one, and gives him time and strength to try again.

According to Schopenhauer, we move across the stage of life stung by appetite and goaded by desire, in pain unceasing, the sole respite from pain, the instant in which desire is lost in satisfaction. To do away with desire is to destroy pain, but it also destroys existence. Desire is lost where the "mouth is stopped with dust," and with death only comes relief from pain.

Thus the Pessimist tells us that "the only reality in life is pain." But surely this is not the truth. He who knows no reality save appetite has never known life at all. The realities in life are love and action; not desire, but the exercise of our appointed functions.

Action follows sensation. The more we have to do the more accurate must be our sensations, the greater the hold environment has upon us. Broader activities demand better knowledge of our surroundings. Greater sensitiveness to external things means greater capacity for pain, hence greater suffering, when the natural channels of effort are closed. Thus arises the hope for nothingness in which many sensitive souls have indulged. With no surroundings at all, or with environment that never varies, there could be no sense-perception. To see nothing, to feel nothing—there could be no demand for action. With no failure of action there could be no weariness. From the varied environment of earthly life spring, through adaptation, the varied powers and varied sensibilities, susceptibilities to joy and pain as well as the rest. The greater the sensitiveness the greater the capacity for suffering. Hence the "quenching of desire," the "turning toward Nirvana, the desire to escape from the hideous bustle of a world in which we are able to take no part, is a natural impulse with the soul which feels but cannot or will not act.

"Can it be, O Christ in Heaven,
That the highest suffer most,
That the strongest wander farthest
And most hopelessly are lost?—

That the mark of rank in Nature
Is capacity for pain,
And the anguish of the singer
Marks the sweetness of the strain?

That this must be so rests in the very nature of things. The most perfect instrument is one most easily thrown out of adjustment. The most highly developed organism is the most exactly fitted to its functions, the one most deeply injured when these functions are altered or suppressed.

Man's sensations and power to act must go together. Man can know nothing that he cannot somehow weave into action. If he fails to do this in one form or another, it is through limitations he has placed on himself. Man cannot suffer for lack of "more worlds to conquer," because his power to conquer worlds is the product of his own 'past life and his own past needs. To weave knowledge into action is the antidote for ennui. To plan, to hope, to do, to accomplish the full measure of our powers, whatever they may be, is to turn away from Nirvana to real life. A useful man, a helpful man, an active man in any sense, even though his, activity be misdirected or harmful, is always a hopeful man.

The feeling that "the only reality in life is pain," is the sign not of philosophical acuteness but of bodily under-vitalization. The nervous system is too feeble for the body it has to move. To act is to make the environment your servant. Its pressure is no longer pain but joy. The concessions which life has made to time and space are the source of life's glory and power.

The function of the nervous system is to carry from the environment to the brain the impressions of truth, that action may be true and safe. Pain and pleasure are both incidental to sound action. The one drives, the other coaxes us toward the path of wisdom. If pain is in excess of joy in our experience, it is because we have wandered from the path of normal activity. By right-doing, we mean that action which makes for "abundance of life," and abundance of life means fulness of joy. "Though life be sad, yet there's joy in the living it" was the word of the ancient Greeks, "who ever with a frolic welcome took the Thunder and the Sunshine."

The life of man is dynamic, not static; not a condition but a movement. "Not enjoyment and not sorrow" is its end or justification. It is a rush of forces, an evolution towards greater activities and higher adjustment, the growth of a stability which shall be ever more unstable. This onward motion is recognized in the pessimistic philosophy of Von Hartmann, as a movement towards ever greater possibilities of pain. With him life is "the supreme blunder of the blind unconscious force" which created man and developed him as the prey of ever-increasing suffering.

But the power to enjoy has grown in like degree, and both joy and pain are subordinated to the power to act. The human will, the power to do, is the real end of the stress and struggle of the ages. However limited its individual action, the will finds its place among the gigantic factors in the evolution of life. It is not the present, but the ultimate, which is truth. Not the unstable and temporary fact but the boundless clashing forces which endlessly throw truths to the surface.

Another source of Pessimism is the reaction from unearned pleasures and from spurious joys. It is the business of the senses to translate realities, to tell the truth about us in terms of human experience. Every real pleasure has its cost in some form of nervous activity. What we get we must earn, if it is to be really ours. Long ago, in the infancy of civilization, man learned that there were drugs in Nature, cell products of the growth or transformation of "our brother organisms, the plants," by whose agency pain was turned to pleasure. By the aid of these outside influences he could clear "today of past regrets and future fears," and strike out from the sad "calendar unborn tomorrow and dead yesterday."

That the joys thus produced had no real objective existence, man was not long in finding out, and it soon appeared that for each subjective pleasure which had no foundation in action, there was a subjective sorrow, likewise unrelated to external things.

But that the pains more than balanced the joys, and that the indulgence in unearned deceptions destroyed sooner or later all capacity for enjoyment, man learned more slowly.

The joys of wine, of opium, of tobacco and of all kindred drugs are mere tricks upon the nervous system. In greater or less degree they destroy its power to tell the truth, and in proportion as they have seemed to bring subjective happiness, so do they bring at last subjective horror and disgust. And this utter soul-weariness of drugs has found its way into literature as the expression of Pessimism.

"The City of the Dreadful Night," for example, does not find its inspiration in the misery of selfish, rushing, crowded London. It is the effect of brandy on the sensitive mind of an exquisite poet. Not the world, but the poet, lies in the "dreadful night" of self-inflicted insomnia. Wherever these subjective nerve influences find expression in literature it is either in an infinite sadness, or in hopeless gloom. James Thompson says in the "City of the Dreadful Night":

"The city is of night but not of sleep;
There sweet sleep is not for the weary brain.
The pitiless hours like years and ages creep—
A night seems termless hell. This dreadful strain

Of thought and consciousness which never ceases,
Or which some moment's stupor but increases."

* * *

"This Time which crawleth like a monstrous snake,
Wounded and slow and very venomous."

* * *

'Lo, as thus prostrate in the dust I write
My heart's deep languor and my soul's sad tears—
But why evoke the spectres of black night
To blot the sunshine of exultant years!

"Because a cold rage seizes one at times
To show the bitter, old and wrinkled truth,
Stripped naked of all vesture that beguiles
False dreams, false hopes, false masks and modes of
youth."

All this, alas, is the inevitable physical outcome of the
attempt to—

"Divorce old, barren Reason from my house
To take the daughter of the vine to spouse."

All subjective happiness due to nerve stimulation is of
the nature of mania. In proportion to its intensity is the
certainty that it will be followed by its subjective
reaction, the "Nuit Blanche," the "dark brown taste," by
the experience of "the difference in the morning." The
only melancholy drugs can drive away is that which they

themselves produce. It is folly to use as a source of pleasure that which lessens activity and vitiates life.

There are many other causes which induce depression of mind and disorder of nerve. Where nerve decay is associated with genius and culture, we shall find some phase of the philosophy of Pessimism. In fact, cheerfulness is not primarily a result of right thinking, but rather the expression of sound nerves and normal vegetative processes. Most of the philosophy of despair, the longing to know the meaning of the unattainable, vanishes with active out-of-door life and the consequent flow of good health. Even a dose of quinine may convert to hopefulness when both sermons and arguments fail.

For a degree of optimism is a necessary accompaniment of health. It is as natural as animal heat, and is the mental reflex of it. Pessimism arises from depression or irritation or failure of the nerves. It is a symptom of lowered vitality expressed in terms of the mind.

There is a philosophical Pessimism, as I have already said, over and above all merely physical conditions, and not dependent on them. But the melancholy Jacques of our ordinary experience either uses some narcotic or stimulant to excess, or else has trouble with his liver or kidneys. "Liver complaint," says Zangwill, "is the Prometheus myth done into modern English." Already historical criticism has shown that the Bloody Assizes had its origin in disease of the bladder, and most forms of vice and cruelty resolve themselves into decay of the nerves. It is natural that degeneration should bring discouragement and disgust. But whatever the causes of

Pessimism, whether arising in speculative philosophy in nervous disease or in personal failure, it can never be wrought into sound and helpful life. To live effectively implies the belief that life is worth living, and no one who leads a worthy life has ever for a moment doubted this.

Such an expression as "worth living" has in fact no real meaning. To act and to love are the twin functions of the human body and soul. To refuse these functions is to make one's self incapable of them. It is in a sense to die while the body is still alive. To refuse these functions is to make misery out of existence, and a life of ennui is doubtless not "worth living."

The philosophy of life is its working hypothesis of action. To hold that all effort is futile, that all knowledge is illusion, and that no result of the human will is worth the pain of calling it into action, is to cut the nerve of effectiveness. In proportion as one really believes this, he becomes a cumberer of the ground. It was said of Oscar McCulloch, an earnest student of human life, that "in whatever part of God's universe he finds himself, he will be a hopeful man, looking forward and not backward, looking upward and not downward, always ready to lend a helping hand, and not afraid to die."

Of like spirit was Robert Louis Stevenson:

"Glad did I live and gladly die,
And I laid me down with a will."

It is through men of this type that the work of civilization has been accomplished, "men of present valor, stalwart, brave iconoclasts." They were men who were content with the order of the universe as it is, and seek only to place their own actions in harmony with this order. They have no complaints to urge against "the goodness and severity of God," nor any futile wish "to remould it nearer to the heart's desire." The "Fanaticism for Veracity" is satisfied with what is. Not the ultimate truth which is God's alone, but the highest attainable truth, is the aim of Science, and to translate Science into Virtue is the goal of civilization.

The third question which Science may ask is the direct one. In what part of the universe are you, and what are you doing? Thoreau says that "there is no hope for you unless this bit of sod under your feet is the sweetest to you in this world—in any world." Why not? Nowhere is the sky so blue, the grass so green, the sunshine so bright, the shade so welcome, as right here, now, today. No other blue sky, nor bright sunshine, nor welcome shade exists for you. Other skies are bright to other men. They have been bright in the past and so will they be again, but yours are here and now. Today is your day and mine, the only day we have, the day in which we play our part. What our part may signify in the great whole we may not understand, but we are here to play it, and now is the time. This we know, it is a part of action, not of whining. It is a part of love, not cynicism. It is for us to express love in terms of human helpfulness. This we know, for we have learned from sad experience that any other course of life leads toward decay and waste.

What, then, are you doing under these blue skies? The thing you do should be for you the most important thing in the world. If you could do something better than you are doing now, everything considered, why are you not doing it?

If every one did the very best he knew, most of the problems of human life would be already settled. If each one did the best he knew, he would be on the highway to greater knowledge, and therefore still better action. The redemption of the world is waiting only for each man to "lend a hand."

It does not matter if the greatest thing for you to do be not in itself great. The best preparation for greatness comes in doing faithfully the little things that lie nearest. The nearest is the greatest in most human lives.

Even washing one's own face may be the greatest present duty. The ascetics of the past, who scorned cleanliness in the search for godliness, became, sometimes, neither clean nor holy. For want of a clean face they lost their souls.

It was Agassiz's strength that he knew the value of today. Never were such bright skies as arched above him; nowhere else were such charming associates, such budding students, such secrets of nature fresh to his hand. His was the buoyant strength of the man who can look the stars in the face because he does his part in the Universe as well as they do theirs. It is the fresh, unspoiled confidence of the natural man, who finds the world a world of action and joy, and time all too short for the fulness of life which it demands. When Agassiz died, "the best friend that ever student had," the students of Harvard "laid a wreath of laurel on his bier, and their manly voices sang a requiem, for he had been a student all his life long, and when he died he was younger than any of them."

Optimism in life is a good working hypothesis, if by optimism we mean the open-eyed faith that force exerted is never lost. Much that calls itself faith is only the blindness of self-satisfaction.

What if there are so many of us in the ranks of humanity? What if the individual be lost in the mass as a pebble cast into the Seven Seas? Would you choose a world so small as to leave room for only you and your satellites? Would you ask for problems of life so tame that even you could grasp them? Would you choose a fibreless Universe to be "remoulded nearer to the heart's desire," in place of the wild, tough, virile, man-making environment from which the Attraction of Gravitation lets none of us escape?

It is not that "I come like water and like wind I go." I am here today, and the moment and the place are real, and my will is itself one of the fates that make and unmake all things. "Every meanest day is the conflux of two eternities," and in this center of all time and space for the moment it is I that stand. Great is Eternity, but it is made up of time. Could we blot out one day in the midst of time, Eternity could be no more. The feebleness of man has its place within the infinite Omnipotence.

It is a question not of hope or despair, but of truth, not of optimism nor of Pessimism, but of wisdom. Wisdom is knowing what to do next; virtue is doing it. Religion is the heart impulse that turns toward the best and highest course of action. "It was my duty to have loved the highest. What does that demand? What have I to do next? Not in infinity, where we can do nothing, but here, today, the greatest day that ever was, for it alone is mine!

What matter is it that time does not end with us? Neither with us does history begin. An Emperor of China once decreed that nothing should be before him, that all history should begin with him. But he could go no farther than his own decree. Who are you that would be Emperor of China?

"The eternal Saki from that bowl hath poured
Millions of bubbles like us and shall pour."

Why not? Should life stop with you? What have you done that you should mark the end of time? If you have played your part in the procession of bubbles, all is well, though the best you can do is to leave the world a little better for the next that follows.

If you have not made life a little richer and its conditions a little more just by your living you have not touched the world. You are indeed a bubble. If some kind friend somewhere "turn down an empty glass," it will be the best monument you deserve. But to have had a friend is to leave the glass not wholly empty, for life is justified in love as well as in action.

The words of Omar need to be read with the rising inflection, and they become the expression of exultant hopefulness.

"The eternal Saki from that bowl hath poured
Millions of bubbles and shall pour!"

Small though we are the story is not all told when we are dead. The huge procession goes on and shall go on, till the secret of the grand symphony of life is reached.

"A single note in the Eternal Song
A perfect Singer hath had need for me."

* * *

"I do rejoice that when of Thee and Me
Men speak no longer, yet not less but more
The Eternal Saki still that bowl shall fill
And ever fairer, clearer bubbles pour."

In the same way we must read with the rising inflection the lines of Tennyson:

"I falter when I firmly trod,
And falling with my weight of cares,
Upon the World's great altar-stairs
That slope through darkness, up to god!"

Read these words with courage, and with the upward turn of the voice at the end. It is no longer in the darkness that we falter. The great altar-stairs of which no man knows the beginning nor the end, do not spring from the mire nor end in the mists. They "slope through darkness up to God," and no one could ask a stronger expression of that robust optimism which must be the mainspring of successful life.